Weight Watch New Complete Cookbook 2024

Easy, Selected and Delicious Recipes to Energize your Mind and Help you Lose Weight

By
Inez Lc. Delgado

Copyright © **Inez Lc. Delgado** 2024

All rights reserved. No part of this publication maybe reproduced, stored or transmitted in any form or by any means, electronic, mechanical, photocopying, recording, scanning, or otherwise without written permission from the author. It is illegal to copy this book, post it to a website, or distribute it by any other means without permission.

Inez Lc. Delgado moral right to be identified as the author of this work.

TABLE OF CONTENTS

Breakfast Recipes 6
- Sweet Cherry Almond Chia Pudding 6
- Smoked Salmon Eggs Benedict 8
- Keto Breakfast Burger with Avocado Buns 10
- Chocolate Avocado Blueberry Muffins 11
- Raspberry-Grapefruit Smoothie 13
- Smoked Salmon And Spinach Breakfast Recipe 14
- Scrambled Eggs With Smoked Salmon Recipe 16
- Berry & Chia Breakfast 17
- Golden Milk Chia Seed Pudding 18

Lunch Recipes 19
- Glowing Spiced Lentil Soup 19
- Kale Pesto Bulgur Salad Recipe 21
- Curried Red Lentil and Swiss Chard Soup 23
- Turkish Scrambled Eggs 25
- Cardamom-Orange Quinoa with Carrots Recipe 26
- Kale, Chickpea and Tomato Stew Recipe 27
- Smoked Salmon Potato Tartine 29
- Kale Caesar Salad with Grilled Chicken Wrap 31
- Roasted Red Pepper and Sweet Potato Soup 32
- Lettuce Wraps with Smoked Trout 34
- Lentil, Beetroot and Hazelnut Salad and a Ginger Dressing 36

Dinner Recipes 38
- Salmon Cakes 38

- Curried Shrimp & Vegetables Recipe 41
- Gut-Healing Salmon & Cauliflower Rice Bowl 42
- Lentil and Chicken Soup with Sweet Potatoes and Escarole 44
- Roasted cauliflower, fennel and ginger soup 46
- Homemade Vegetarian Chili 47
- Baked Tilapia Recipe with Pecan Rosemary Topping 50
- Turkey & Quinoa Stuffed Peppers 52
- Italian Stuffed Peppers 54
- Mediterranean Tuna-Spinach Salad 56

Desserts Recipes 57
- Frozen Blueberry Bites 57
- One-Ingredient Watermelon Sorbet 58
- Apple Chips 59
- Strawberry-Orange Sorbet 61
- Paleo Pineapple Upside Down Cake 62
- Chocolate Cherry Chia Pudding 63

Smoothies and Drinks 64
- Anti-Inflammatory Pumpkin Smoothie 64
- Anti-Inflammatory Turmeric Ginger Green Smoothie for Weight Loss 65
- Anti-Inflammatory Blueberry Smoothie 66
- Food Babe's Ginger Berry Anti-Inflammatory Smoothie 67
- Anti-Inflammatory Smoothie 68
- Golden Milk Protein Smoothie 69

Snacks Recipes 70
- Ginger Fried Cabbage and Carrots 70

Turmeric Coconut Flour Muffins Recipe 71

Baked Veggie Turmeric Nuggets (Freeze-Friendly) 72

AIP / Paleo Sweet n' Sour Hibiscus Ginger Gelatin Gummies ... 73

Vanilla Turmeric Orange Juice 74

Spicy Tuna Rolls 75

Vegetarian Recipes 76

Thai Coconut Soup with Bok Choy & Mushrooms 76

Anti-Inflammatory Soup (GF/DF) 78

Turmeric Latte 80

Turmeric Roasted Cauliflower 81

Pesto Broccoli Sweet Potato Rice Casserole 82

BREAKFAST RECIPES
Sweet Cherry Almond Chia Pudding

Prep/Cook Time: 20 mins, Servings: 4 - 1 cup
PointValues: 8

Ingredients

- 2 cps whole sweet cherries, pitted (fresh or frozen) weighing 10 oz & 1 Tspoon almond extract
- 1 Tspoon vanilla extract & 1/8 Teaspoon sea salt
- 3/4 cup chia seeds & 1/2 cup hemp seeds
- 1 - 13.5 oz can coconut milk & 1/4 cp maple syrup

For Topping:

- 4 cps halved & pitted fresh or frozen cherries

Instructions

- At first Combine in a blender the 2 cups of cherries, coconut milk, maple syrup, extracts of almond and vanilla, and sea salt. Mix until it is smooth.
- Next Add the seeds of chia and hemp and blend at low to combine.
- Then Pour into refrigerated containers for storage. For 1 cup of chia pudding in each bowl, I used 1-pint containers and filled them halfway.

- Before topping with fresh or frozen cherries, let the chia pudding set up in the fridge for 1 hour. If you immediately try to top the fruit pudding, the fruit will sink into the pudding.
- Finally The puddings are refrigerated for 4-5 days.rated.

Nutrition Info

Calories 242kcal Calories from fat 180, Total Fat 29g, Protein 9g

Smoked Salmon Eggs Benedict

Prep/Cook Time: 40 minutes, Servings: 2
Point Values: 17

Ingredients

- 4 tabsps cream cheese & 3 oz smoked salmon (salmon lox)
- 2 teaspoons capers & 4 large eggs
- 2 English muffins, cut in half, Thinly sliced red onion & A pinch of black pepper

Lemony Hollandaise Sauce

- 2 large egg yolks & 2 tbspoons water
- 2 tablespoons butter (use ghee for Whole30 + paleo), 2 tspoons fresh lemon juice & A pinch of salt

Instructions

- At first Start by making the sauce from the Hollandaise. Next In a small frying pan, add the egg yolks and water. Then Place the pan 2 inches above a medium - high component and whisk the eggs until they are moist and frothy. Add the butter to the pan and whisk until the hollandaise is thick. Do not put the pan on the item! Whisk in a tablespoon of salt and lemon juice and set aside the pan.
- After that Place on high heat a medium-sized pot of water on the stove.
- The English muffins are lightly toasted either in a toaster or by frying them on their cut sides in a little

butter. Place them on the serving plates and spread the cream cheese on top. Divide between them the smoked salmon.
- While the water is boiling, reduce the heat to simmer gently. Crack the eggs at once and allow them to cook for four minutes. Use a slotted spoon to extract them from the pot and place one egg over each English muffin.
- Pour over the eggs the hollandaise sauce and top with a few red onion slices, some capers and a little black pepper.
- FinallyToss few handfuls of baby arugula with a drizzle of olive oil and put the salad next to the benedict eggs if you are serving this with arugula.

Nutrition Info

Calories 418kcal Calories from fat 336, Total Fat 44g, Saturated Fat 9g, Cholesterol 29mg, Sodium 56mg, Carbohydrate 33g, Dietary Fiber 4g, Sugars 9g, Protein 22g

Keto Breakfast Burger with Avocado Buns

Prep/Cook Time: 20 mins, Servings: 1
Point Values: 39

Ingredients

- 1 tomato slice & 1 lettuce leaf
- 1 ripe avocado & 1 egg
- 2 bacon rashers & 1 red onion slice
- 1 T Paleo mayonnaise, Sea salt, to taste & Sesame seeds, for garnish

Instructions

- At first Put the bacon rashers on a cold frying pan. Switch on the stove and start to fry the bacon. Next Flip it with a fork as bacon beings curl. Continue to cook the bacon until it becomes crispy.
- Then Take away the bacon from the pan and use the bacon fat to cook the egg in the same pan. Cook, but the yolk is still runny, until the white is set.
- Slice in half the size of the avocados. Remove the pit and scoop it out of your skin using a spoon.
- Fill the hole where Paleo mayonnaise used to be in the bowl.
- Tomato, lettuce, onion, bacon, and fried egg plate.
- Season with salt from the sea.
- Top with the avocado's second half.
- Finally Sprinkle with seeds of sesame.

Nutrition Info

84 grams of protein, 6 grams of carbohydrates, 121 grams of fat

Chocolate Avocado Blueberry Muffins

These delicious Paleo muffins are made of strawberries, blueberries and dark chocolate-an antioxidant fantasy.

Prep/Cook Time:28 mins, Servings:9 muffins
Point Values: 7

Ingredients

- ¼ ts salt, 1/4 cp raw cacao powder + 1 T & ¼ cup fresh blueberries
- 2 T dark chocolate chips & 2 t baking powder
- 2 T coconut flour & 2 large eggs, room temperature
- 1 small avocado, ripe & 1/3 cup coconut sugar
- 1 cup almond flour & ½ cup unsweetened almond milk

Instructions

- First Oven preheat to 375 ° F. Prepare a muffin tin with coconut oil muffin liners or grease.
- Next In the blender with 1 tablespoon of cacao powder, put eggs, avocado, sugar and salt. Then Mix up until the avocado is completely broken down and the mixture looks like a smooth pudding.
- Sift 1/4 cup of cocoa powder, baking powder, coconut flour and almond flour together in a small bowl.
- Attach the almond milk to the liquid mixture and add in dry ingredients gradually. Mix until mixed together-don't overmix!
- Fold with chocolate chips and blueberries.

- o Move the batter to the prepared muffin tin, equally dividing the batter between 9 cavities.
- o Bake until a toothpick inserted in the middle of a muffin comes out clean for 18 minutes.
- o Take away the muffins from the tin and cool down to a wire baking rack.
- o Finally Save for one week in the fridge or for up to one month in the freezer.

Nutrition Info

Calories 284kcal Calories from fat 150, Total Fat 9g, Saturated Fat 16g, Cholesterol 12mg, Sodium 11mg, Carbohydrate 33g, Sugars 8g, Protein 11g

Raspberry-Grapefruit Smoothie

Prep/Cook Time: 5 mins, Serves 1
Point Values: 7

Ingredients

- 1 pink grapefruit Juice
- 1 banana peeled & sliced (fresh or frozen)
- 1 cp raspberries (fresh or frozen)

Instructions

o Put all ingredients in a blender thenthen process until smooth.

Nutrition Info

245 calories, 60 grams of carbs, 1 gram of fat, and 3 grams of protein.

Smoked Salmon And Spinach Breakfast Recipe

Prep/Cook: 50 min, Serves: 4
Point Values: 8

Ingredients

- 1/2 onion, sliced & 2 cups fresh baby spinach
- 1 garlic clove, minced & 1/2 tsp. onion powder
- 1/2 tsp. garlic powder & 4 eggs
- 8 ounces. smoked salmon, sliced & 2 russet/sweet potatoes, peeled and diced
- 1/2 cup mushrooms, sliced & 1/4 tsp. paprika
- 2 tbsp. ghee, 2 tbsp. olive oil & Sea salt and freshly ground black pepper

Instructions

- At forst Oven preheat to 425 F.
- Next Dice the potatoes, add olive oil, onion powder, paprika, garlic powder and season to taste.
- Then Put the potatoes on a baking dish and cook at halfway point in the oven for 25 to 30 minutes.
- After that Bring a bowl of water over high heat to a boil.
- In the boiling water, add the eggs, turn off the heat and cook for 6 to 7 minutes.
- Drain the water over the eggs and run cold water; peel and set aside the eggs.
- Melt the ghee and add the onion and garlic over medium - high heat.

- Cook 1 to 2 minutes before adding the sliced mushrooms.
- Season to taste and cook for 4 to 5 minutes until all is smooth.
- Attach the spinach and cook for 1 to 2 minutes until wilted.
- Finally Serve the potatoes, filled with the mixture of spinach-mushroom, cheese, and smoked salmon.

Nutrition Info

Protein: 17g, Carbs: 16g, Fat: 20g

Scrambled Eggs With Smoked Salmon Recipe

Prep/Cooking time: 18 min, Servings: 2

Point Values: 9

Ingredients

- 4 eggs; & 4 slices smoked salmon, chopped;
- 2 tbsp. coconut milk; & Fresh chives, finely chopped;
- Cooking fat; & Sea salt and freshly ground black pepper;

Instructions

- At first Whisk the eggs, milk of coconut, and fresh chives in a bowl. Taste the season.
- Next In a skillet, melt some cooking fat and add the eggs.
- Then When baking, scramble the eggs.
- Adding the smoked salmon and cook for 1 or 2 minutes when the eggs begin to settle.
- Finally Serve on top with more sprinkled chives.

Nutrition Info

Calories: 217k Protein: 44g, Carbs: 1g, Fat: 20g

Berry & Chia Breakfast

Prep/Cook Time: 40 mins, Servings: 1
Point Values: 11

Ingredient

- 3 teabsp desiccated coconut, unsweetened & 3 teabsp chia seeds
- 1 cup / 125 g fresh or thawed frozen raspberries & 1 pinch ground vanilla
- 1 cup / 240 ml plant milk (we prefer almond, coconut or oat milk)

Topping
- nut butter
- hemp seeds
- kiwi
- fresh mint

Instructions

o At first Use a fork to mash the berries in a bowl. Next Remove and mix the seeds of vanilla, coconut and chia. Garnish with milk and blend. Then Put aside to chill in the fridge for at least 30 minutes or overnight. Finally Serve with nut butter, hemp seeds, berries and mint in a bowl or jar.

Nutrition Info: Calories 130kcal, Total Fat 34g, Saturated Fat 9g, Cholesterol 22mg, Protein 20g

Golden Milk Chia Seed Pudding

Prep/Cook Time: 6 hrs, Serves:4
Point Values: 5

Ingredients

- ½ t ground cinnamon & ½ t ground ginger
- ½ cup chia seeds & 4 cups full-fat coconut milk
- 3 T honey & 1 t vanilla extract
- 1 t ground turmeric & ¾ cup coconut yogurt, for topping
- 1 cup fresh mixed berries, for garnishing & ¼ cup toasted coconut chips, for garnishing

Instructions

- At first Combine in a large mixing bowl the coconut milk, sugar, vanilla extract, turmeric, cinnamon, and ground ginger. Next Combine well, producing a bright yellow liquid.
- Then mix well in the chia seeds and set aside for 5 minutes. Stir it around once again when necessary.
- Cover that bowl and let it cool down for at least 6 hours or overnight in the refrigerator. This will allow the seeds of chia to plump and give a thick consistency of pudding to the mix.
- Finally Divide chia seed pudding into 4 serving glasses evenly, then finish with a coconut yogurt dollop. Garnish with coconut chips and mixed berries.

Nutrition Info

Calories 333kcal Calories from fat 204, Total Fat 4g, Saturated Fat 7g, Cholesterol 4mg, Sodium 8mg, Carbohydrate 22g, Sugars 8g, Dietary Fiber 3g, Protein 24g

LUNCH RECIPES

Glowing Spiced Lentil Soup

Prep/Cook Time: 35 mins, Servings: 7 cups (1.65 litres)
Point Values: 9

Ingredients:

- 1/4 teaspoon ground cardamom & 1 (15-oz/398 mL) can diced tomatoes, with juices
- 1 (15-oz/398 mL) can full-fat coconut milk* & 3/4 cup (140 grams) uncooked red lentils, rinsed and drained
- 3 1/2 cups (875 mL) low-sodium vegetable broth & 1/2 tspoon fine sea salt, or to taste
- Freshly ground black pepper, to taste & 1 1/2 tabspns extra-virgin olive oil
- 2 cups (280 grams) diced onion (1 medium/large) & 2 large garlic cloves, minced
- 2 teaspoons ground turmeric & 1 1/2 teaspoons ground cumin
- 1/2 teaspoon cinnamon & Red pepper flakes/cayenne pepper, to taste (for a kick of heat!)
- 1 (5-oz/140-gram) package baby spinach & 2 tspns fresh lime juice, or more to taste

Instructions

- At first Place the butter, onion and garlic in a large pot. For 4 to 5 minutes, next add a pinch of salt, stir, and sauté over medium heat until the onion softens.

- Then blend, add the turmeric, cumin, cinnamon and cardamom. Continue to cook, until fragrant, for about 1 minute.
- After that Add the diced tomatoes, whole can of coconut milk, red lentils, broth, salt, and plenty of pepper. If needed, add red pepper flakes or cayenne to taste. Shake to mix. Increase the heat to high and bring it to a low boil.
- Reduce the heat to medium-high once it boils, and simmer uncovered for about 18 to 22 minutes until the lentils are tender & fluffy.
- Finally Turn off the heat and whisk until wilted in the spinach. Add to taste the lime juice. If needed, try and add more salt and pepper. Using toasted bread and lime wedges to serve in bowls.

Nutrition Info

Calories: 182, Fat: 24g, Sodium: 36mg, Carbohydrates: 31g, Fiber: 22g, Sugar: 1.4g, Protein: 11g

Kale Pesto Bulgur Salad Recipe

Prep/Cook Time: 40 mins, Serves 4-6
Point Values: 5

Ingredients

- 1 1/2 cups bulgur & 1 tsp. kosher salt, divided, plus more to taste
- 1 pint grape tomatoes, halved & 1/2 pnds green beans, trimmed & cut into bite-sized pieces
- 1/4 cup plus 3 Tbsp. sliced almonds, toasted, plus more for garnish & 1 garlic clove
- 1 cup stemmed and thinly sliced lacinato kale (from about 1/2 bunch) & 1/2 cup packed basil leaves
- 1/4 packed flat-leaf parsley & 3 Tbsp. sliced almonds
- 1/4 cup extra-virgin olive oil & 1/4 cp lemon juice (about 2 lemons)
- 1/2 tsp. kosher salt & 1/4 tsp. ground black pepper

Instructions

To make salad:

- Soak the bulgur and 1/2 tsp in a large bowl. Heat overnight in three cups of water. If required, drain. (or, take 3 cups of water to a boil, then pour over bulgur in a heat-proof bowl, cover, and let sit for 25 minutes.

To make pesto:

- Pulse the garlic until it is sliced in a food processor equipped with a metal blade. Add the almonds to the kale, basil, parsley and 1/4 cup and pulse until finely chopped. Add the remaining 1/2 tsp of oil, lemon juice. Season with salt, pepper and purée until smooth.
- Move the pesto to the bulgur pan. Remove onions, green beans, and 3 Tbsp remaining. A combination of almonds and toss well. Garnish and serve with extra almonds.

Nutrition Info

Calories: 234, Fat: 8g, Sodium: 44mg, Carbohydrates: 24g, Fiber: 13g, Sugar: 1.2g, Protein: 18g

Curried Red Lentil and Swiss Chard Soup

Prep/Cook Time: 30 mins, Servings: 6
Point Values: 10

Ingredients

- 1 bunch (1-pounds) Swiss chard , tough stalks removed, coarsely chopped & 2 cps (about 14 ounces) dried red lentils
- 1 can (15-ounce) chickpeas , rinsed and drained & 1 teaspoon salt
- 2 tablespoons olive oil & 1 large onion , thinly sliced
- 5 teaspoons curry powder & 1/4 teaspoon ground red pepper (cayenne)
- 5 cups vegetable broth & 6 tbspoons thick Greek yogurt , thinned with 2 tbs water
- 1 red or green jalapeño chili , stemmed and thinly sliced & 1 lime , cut into 6 wedges

Instructions

- At first Heat the oil over medium heat in a big, heavy saucepan. Next Add onion; cook, stirring frequently, about 10 minutes until slightly golden. Then Incorporate curry and red pepper. Increase that heat and bring to a boil, stirring until chard is wilted, add 4 cups of broth and chard.
- After that Stir in chickpeas and lentils. Reduce heat to low, cover it and simmer for 16 to 18 minutes until lentils are tender, stirring twice.
- In the next step Remove from heat. In the blender or food processor, puree half the soup (about 4 cups);

return the puree to the bowl. Add remaining 1 cup of broth and salt and steam for 2 minutes over low heat.
- Finally Divide the soup between six bowls. Drizzle over each serving about 1 tablespoon of thin yogurt. Garnish with some jalapeño slices and a lime wedge.

Nutrition Info: Calories 346 , 21 grams fat, 18 grams protein, 23 grams carbohydrates.

Turkish Scrambled Eggs

Prep/Cook Time: 35 minutes, Serves 4
Point Values: 10

Ingredients

- 2 Tabsp. canola or olive oil & 3 scallions, finely chopped
- 1 teasp. crushed red pepper flakes & 6 eggs, beaten
- 2 large red bell peppers, seeded then finely chopped & 4 ounces crumbled Feta cheese (optional)
- 1/2 teasp. kosher salt & 2 to 4 ripe tomatoes, diced (1 pound)
- 1/4 teasp. ground black pepper & 2 Tabsp. chopped fresh parsley
- Green olives, for garnish (optional) & 4 whole grain pitas, for serving

Instructions

- First Heat oil over medium to high heat in a medium skillet. Next Attach the scallions and cook for about 2 minutes until tender. Then Continue to cook for 5 minutes. Add tomatoes and flakes of red pepper and sauté until some of the tomato liquid starts to evaporate.
- Finally Add the eggs and feta (if used) and scramble until the eggs are fully cooked and the vegetables are coated, stirring constantly. Season to taste with salt and pepper. Stir in parsley and remove from heat. Serve on the side with green olives (if used) and pitas of whole grain.

Nutrition Info: 346 calories, 18 grams protein, 21 grams fat, 23 grams carbohydrates.

Cardamom-Orange Quinoa with Carrots Recipe

Prep/Cook Time: 30 mins, Servings: 4
Point Values: 8

Ingredients

- 1 lb carrots, peeled and sliced & 1/3 cup golden raisins
- One 1-inch piece fresh ginger, peeled then minced & 2 oranges
- 1 cup red, white or black quinoa, rinsed well under cold water & 2 1/2 cups chicken broth, vegetable broth or bone broth
- 1 tsp. ground cardamom, 1/2 tsp. salt & 1/2 tsp. freshly ground black pepper

Instructions

- At first Zest the oranges and keep the fruit in reserve
- Next In a slow cooker, mix well the quinoa, broth, carrots, raisins, ginger, cardamom, cinnamon, black pepper, and orange zest.
- Then Cover the slow cooker and cook until the quinoa is tender in the low setting for 3 to 3 1/2 hours. Cut the peel from the oranges using a chef's knife. Work on a large bowl to separate the oranges.
- After that Hold the peeled orange in your hand, use a small paring knife to slice between the white orange membranes to free the segments and let them fall into the bowl as you continue to the next segment
- In the next step Repeat with the rest of the orange In cups, spoon the quinoa and cover each serving with a few fragments of orange.
- Then Serve right away.

Nutrition Info

170 calories, 5 g protein, 3 g fat (1 g saturated fat), 1 mg cholesterol, 31 g carbohydrates, 11 g sugars, 5 g fiber, 230 mg sodium

Kale, Chickpea and Tomato Stew Recipe

Prep/Cook Time: 40 minutes, Serves 4
Point Values: 3

Ingredients

- 4 Tbsp. olive oil, divided & 1 medium onion, cut into eighths
- 1 1/4 tsp. kosher salt, divided & 6 garlic cloves, thinly sliced
- 1/4 tsp. crushed red pepper flakes & 3/4 pound kale, stems removed & leaves coarsely chopped
- 1 pound tomatoes (about 3 medium), cored and chopped & 2 (15-ounce) cans chickpeas, drained and rinsed
- 1 cup vegetable stock & 4 large eggs

Instructions

- At first Heat 2 Tbsp in a big pan. Oil at medium at low heat. Next Add 1/4 tsp of onion. Salt and cook for about 7 minutes until tender. Then Remove flakes of garlic and red pepper and cook for another 2 minutes. Remove kale and stir for about 2 minutes until wilted. Add tomatoes, chickpeas and stock; cook over medium heat until the tomatoes break down for about 10 minutes. 3/4 tsp salt to season.
- Finally Heat remaining 2 Tbsp in a large nonstick skillet. Medium heat oil. Crack 2 eggs and cook for about 3 minutes until slightly crisp on the bottom and white. Take to a plate and repeat with 2 eggs left over.

Stew spoon into 4 shallow bowls, each with a fried egg on top, sprinkle with 1/4 tsp remaining salt and serve.

Nutrition Info: Calories: 188, Fat: 3.8g, Sodium: 145mg, Carbohydrates: 3g, Fiber: 3.3g, Sugar: 12g, Protein: 25g

Smoked Salmon Potato Tartine

Prep/Cook Time: 45 minutes, 2 Servings
Point Values: 3

Ingredients

Potato Tartine:

- 1 large russet potato, peeled & grated lengthwise
- 2 tbspoons clarified butter (or other neutral flavored oil), salt & pepper

Toppings:

- 1/2 garlic clove, finely minced & zest of half a lemon
- 1/2 hard boiled egg, finely chopped & thinly sliced smoked salmon
- 2 tablespoons drained capers & 2 tablespoons finely chopped red onion
- 4ounces soft goat cheese, at room temperature, 1 1/2 tbspoons finely minced chives & finely minced chives (for garnish)

Instructions

Assemble Toppings:

- At first In a small bowl, mix goat's cheese, lemon zest and garlic. Next Season to taste with salt and pepper. Stir gently in the fresh chives. Put it aside.
- Finally Season the chopped onion with salt and the hard-boiled egg.

Prepare Potato Tartine:
- First Work quickly (as the potato starts to oxidize quickly), grate the potato (lengthwise) into a large one using a grater's large holes. Next To remove any excess water, squeeze the potatoes over the sink. Then Season with salt and pepper and toss generously.
- Heat clarified butter over medium - high heat in an 8-10-inch non-stick skillet. When it hot, add the grated potato and shape roughly to a large circle using a spatula.
- To compact, cover and cook gently for 8-10 minutes or until the bottom is golden brown, press the mixture with back of a spoon.
- Flip to the other side carefully and cook for another 8-10 minutes or until golden brown and crispy.
- Remove from the rack to cool and allow to cool until the temperature is barely lukewarm or room.
- Assemble Tartine: spread the goat cheese mixture over the top once the potato cake has cooled. Spoon directly over the smoked salmon and scatter with the red onion, hard-boiled egg, and capers. Garnish with chives that have been freshly cut.
- Finally Cut into wedges and serve as soon as possible.

Nutrition Info

Calories: 304, Fat: 8g, Sodium: 115mg, Carbohydrates: 6g, Fiber: 2g, Sugar: 1.2g, Protein: 4.7g

Kale Caesar Salad with Grilled Chicken Wrap

Prep/Cook Time: 15 minute(s), Servings: 2
Point Values: 5

Ingredients

- 1 cup cherry tomatoes, quartered & 3/4 cup finely shredded Parmesan cheese
- ½ coddled egg (cooked about 1 minute) & 1 clove garlic, minced
- 8 oz grilled chicken, thinly sliced & 6 cups curly kale, cut into bite sized pieces
- 1/2 teaspoon Dijon mustard & 1 teaspoon honey or agave
- 1/8 cup fresh lemon juice & 1/8 cup olive oil
- Kosher salt and freshly ground black pepper & 2 Lavash flat breads or two large tortillas

Instructions

- First Mix half of a coddled potato, chopped garlic, mustard, butter, lemon juice and olive oil together in a pan. Next Whisk until a dressing has been created. Then Season with salt and pepper to taste.
- After that Add the tomatoes of broccoli, chicken and cherry and toss to coat with the shredded parmesan dressing and 1/4 cup.
- Layer the two flatbreads of the lavash. Spread the salad evenly over the two wraps and sprinkle with 1/4 cup of parmesan each.
- Finally Roll up and slice half of the wraps. Eat right away

Nutrition Info

Calories: 190, Fat: 6g, Sodium: 120mg, Carbohydrates: 6g, Fiber: 3g, Sugar: 1.4g, Protein: 30g

Roasted Red Pepper and Sweet Potato Soup

Prep/Cook Time: 55 minutes, 6 servings
Point Values: 3

Ingredients

- 1 can (4 oz) diced green chiles & 2 tspoons ground cumin
- 1 tspoon salt & 1 tspoon ground coriander
- 3 to 4 cups peeled, cubed sweet potatoes & 2 tblespoons olive oil
- 2 medium onions, chopped & 1 jar (12ounces) roasted red peppers, chopped, liquid reserved
- 4 cups vegetable broth & 2 tblespns minced fresh cilantro
- 1 tblespn lemon juice & 4 oz cream cheese, cubed

Instructions

- At first Heat the olive oil over medium - high heat in a large soup pot or Dutch oven. Next Incorporate the onion and cook until soft. Add chilies, cumin, salt and coriander in the red peppers. Cook for about 1-2 minutes.
- Then In the roasted red peppers, sweet potatoes and vegetable broth, add the reserved juice. Take to a boil, then lower heat and cover. Cook for 10-15 minutes until the potatoes are tender. Stir in the juice of the coriander and the lemon. Let the soup cool down a little bit.

- Finally Layer half of the soup with the cream cheese in a blender. Process until smooth, then add back and heat through the soup pot. Season with extra salt if necessary.

Nutrition Info

Calories: 278, Fat: 9g, Protein: 11g

Lettuce Wraps with Smoked Trout

Prep/Cook Time: 45 mins, 4 servings
Point Values: 13

Ingredients

- 1/2 unpeeled English hothouse cucumber (don't remove seeds) & 1/4 cp thinly sliced shallots
- 1/4 cp thinly sliced jalapeño chiles with seeds (preferably red; about 2 large) & 2 4.5-oz packages skinless smoked trout fillets, broken into bite-size pieces (upto 2 cups)
- 2 tblpoons fresh lime juice or unseasoned rice vinegar & 1 tbspoon sugar
- 1 tbspoon fish sauce (such as nam pla or nuoc nam) & 2 medium carrots, peeled
- 1 cp diced grape tomatoes & 1/3 cp Asian sweet chili sauce
- 1/4 cp finely chopped lightly salted dry-roasted peanuts & 1/2 cup whole fresh mint leaves
- 1/2 cup small whole fresh basil leaves & 16 small to medium inner leaves of romaine lettuce (from about 2 hearts of romaine)

Instructions

- At first Rasp carrots and cucumber lengthwise into ribbons using vegetable peeler. Next Cut ribbons into sections of 3 inches, then cut sections into strips of match-stick length. Set in a big bowl. Add shallots,

- jalapeños, lime juice, sugar and fish sauce and marinate at room temperature for 30 minutes.
- Then Add bits of trout and tomatoes to the mixture of vegetables and blend together. Transfer the mixture of trout and vegetables to the large strainer and drain the liquid. Return the mixture of trout and vegetable to the same bowl; add mint and basil and mix.
- Finally Arrange the leaves of lettuce on the large plate. Divide the lettuce leaves in the salad of the broccoli. Sprinkle each salad with sweet chili sauce and sprinkle with peanuts.

Nutrition Info

Calories 423, Carbohydrates 60 g, Fat 12 g, Protein 33 g, Saturated Fat 2 g, Sodium 1245 mg

Lentil, Beetroot and Hazelnut Salad and a Ginger Dressing

Prep/Cook Time: 10 minutes, Serves 2–3
Point Values: 23

Ingredients

For the salad:

- 2 spring onions, finely sliced & 2 tablepoons hazelnuts, roughly chopped
- A handful of fresh mint, roughly chopped & A handful of fresh parsley, roughly chopped & 1 cup Puy lentils, rinsed
- 2 3/4 cup filtered water, Sea salt & 3 cooked beetroot, cut into small cubes

For the ginger dressing:

- 1 teaspoon Dijon mustard & 1 tablespoon apple cider vinegar
- 3/4 inch cube of fresh ginger, peeled and roughly chopped, 6 tbpoons olive oil & Pinch of sea salt then freshly ground black pepper

Instructions

- At first Place them in a saucepan for the lentils, cover with water, bring the heat to the boil then simmer for about 15 minutes–20 minutes, or until all liquid has evaporated and lentils are not mushy & still with a bite.

- Next Transfer them to a big bowl as soon as the lentils are cooked and leave to cool.
- Then Adding the beetroot, hazelnuts, spring onions, and herbs once the lentils are cool and stir until all is mixed.
- After that Put the ginger, oil, mustard and vinegar in a bowl for the dressing and mix until combined with a handheld blender.
- Finally Drizzle and serve the dressing over the salad.

Nutritional Info

Calories 815, Carbohydrates 78 g, Fat 46 g, Protein 28 g, Saturated Fat 6 g, Sodium 1486 mg

DINNER RECIPES

Salmon Cakes

Prep/Cook Time: 2 hr 20 min, 5 servings
Point Values: 5

Ingredients

- 1/2 pound fresh salmon & Good olive oil
- Kosher salt and freshly ground black pepper & 4 tablespoons unsalted butter
- 3/4 cup small-diced red onion (1 small onion) & 1 1/2 cups small-diced celery (4 stalks)
- 1/2 cup small-diced red bell pepper (1 small pepper) & 1/2 cup small-diced yellow bell pepper (1 small pepper)
- 1/4 cup minced fresh flat-leaf parsley & 1 tablespoon capers, drained
- 1/4 teaspoon hot sauce (recommended: Tabasco) & 1/2 teaspoon Worcestershire sauce
- 1 1/2 teaspoons crab boil seasoning (recommended: Old Bay) & 3 slices stale bread, crusts removed
- 1/2 cup good mayonnaise , 2 teaspoons Dijon mustard & 2 extra-large eggs, lightly beaten

Instructions

- o At first Preheat the oven to 350 degrees F.

- Next Place the salmon on a sheet pan, skin side down. Brush with olive oil and sprinkle with salt and pepper. Then Roast for 15 to 20 minutes, until just cooked. Remove from the oven and cover tightly with aluminum foil. Allow to rest for 10 minutes and refrigerate until cold.
- Meanwhile, place 2 tablespoons of the butter, 2 tablespoons olive oil, the onion, celery, red and yellow bell peppers, parsley, capers, hot sauce, Worcestershire sauce, crab boil seasoning, 1/2 teaspoon salt, and 1/2 teaspoon pepper in a large saute pan over medium-low heat and cook until the vegetables are soft, approximately 15 to 20 minutes. Cool to room temperature.
- Break the bread slices in pieces and process the bread in a food processor fitted with a steel blade. You should have about 1 cup of bread crumbs. Place the bread crumbs on a sheet pan and toast in the oven for 5 minutes until lightly browned, tossing occasionally.
- Flake the chilled salmon into a large bowl. Add the bread crumbs, mayonnaise, mustard, and eggs. Add the vegetable mixture and mix well. Cover and chill in the refrigerator for 30 minutes. Shape into 10 (2 1/2 to 3-ounce) cakes.
- Finally Heat the remaining 2 tablespoons butter and 2 tablespoons olive oil in a large saute pan over medium heat. In batches, add the salmon cakes and fry for 3 to 4 minutes on each side, until browned. Drain on paper towels; keep them warm in a preheated 250 degree F oven and serve hot.

Nutrition Info

Calories: 262, Fat: 8.2g, Carbohydrates: 9g, Sugar: 3.3g, Fiber: 9.2g, Protein: 34g

Curried Shrimp & Vegetables Recipe

Prep/Cook Time: 25 minutes, Servings 4

Point Values: 9

Ingredients

- 3 TBSP butter or coconut oil & 1 onion sliced
- 1 cup coconut milk & 1-3 tsp curry powder
- 1 lb shrimp tails removed & 1 bag frozen cauliflower or other frozen veggies of choice

Instructions

- At first Melt butter or oil in skillet and add sliced onion.
- Next Saute onion until it is slightly soft.
- Meanwhile, steam vegetables.
- When onion is softened add coconut milk, curry seasoning, and other spices if desired.
- After that Cook a couple minutes to incorporate flavors.
- In the next step Add thawed shrimp and cook approximately 5 minutes or until shrimp are cooked
- Finally Serve with steamed veggies of choice topped with butter and salad with homemade dressing.

Nutrition Info

Calories: 332kcal, Carbohydrates: 11.2g, Protein: 23.9g, Fat: 22.7g, Saturated Fat: 16.7g, Cholesterol: 208mg

Gut-Healing Salmon & Cauliflower Rice Bowl

Prep/Cook Time: 30 mins, 1 hour 20 mins, Serves 2
Point Values: 11

Ingredients

- 2 salmon fillets, sustainably sourced or organic & 10 to 12 Brussels sprouts, chopped in half
- 1 bunch kale, washed and shredded & ½ head cauliflower, pulsed into cauliflower rice (you can use a whole cauliflower head if you wish)
- 3 tablespoons olive or coconut oil , 1 teaspoon curry powder & Himalayan salt

For marinade

- ¼ cup tamari sauce & 1 teaspoon Dijon mustard
- 1 teaspoon sesame oil , 1 teaspoon honey or maple syrup (optional) & 1 tablespoon sesame seeds

Instructions

- At first Preheat oven to 350°F.
- Next Line a baking tray and add chopped Brussels sprouts. Then Coat with 1 tablespoon oil and season with salt. Add to oven and roast for 20 minutes.
- Meanwhile, make marinade by combining all ingredients in a bowl and whisking until combined.
- Remove Brussels sprouts after 20 minutes and add salmon fillets to the baking tray. Spoon marinade over

salmon fillets and return to oven for a further 13 to 15 minutes, or until salmon is cooked to your liking.
- While salmon is cooking, heat a pan over medium-high heat and add 1 tablespoon oil. Add kale and sauté until wilted (2 to 3 minutes). Remove from pan and set aside.
- Heat remaining oil in pan and add cauliflower rice. Season with 1 teaspoon curry powder and salt and sauté until cooked (2 to 3 minutes).
- Finally Remove salmon and Brussels sprouts from oven and divide into two bowls. Add sautéed kale and cauliflower rice to bowls.

Nutrition Info

Calories: 304kcal, Carbohydrates: 16.2g, Protein: 23g, Fat: 27g, Saturated Fat: 16g, Cholesterol: 167mg

Lentil and Chicken Soup with Sweet Potatoes and Escarole

Prep/Cook Time: 35 minutes, 4–6 servings
Point Values: 14

Ingredients

- 1 cooked chicken carcass (from 1 store-bought rotisserie chicken or homemade roast chicken) & 1 lb. sweet potatoes (about 2 medium), peeled, cut into 1" pieces
- 3/4 cup French lentils (about 5 oz.), rinsed & 1 tsp. kosher salt, plus more
- 2 Tbsp. extra-virgin olive oil & 10 celery stalks, sliced on the bias into 1/4" slices
- 6 garlic cloves, thinly sliced & 1 1/2 cups shredded cooked chicken (from 1/2 of a store-bought rotisserie chicken or homemade roast chicken)
- 1/2 head escarole, cut into bite-size pieces , 1/2 cup finely chopped dill & 2 Tbsp. fresh lemon juice

Instructions

- At first Place chicken carcass, potatoes, lentils, and 1 tsp. salt in a large pot. Next Cover with 8 cups water. Then Bring to a boil over high heat, skimming off any foam, then reduce heat to medium-low and simmer until potatoes are fork tender and lentils are cooked through, 10–12 minutes. Discard chicken carcass.
- Meanwhile, heat oil in a large heavy skillet over medium-high. Add celery and garlic and cook, stirring

often, until celery and garlic are lightly golden brown and tender, about 12 minutes.
- Finally Stir celery, garlic, shredded chicken, and escarole into soup and cook, stirring occasionally, until escarole is wilted, about 5 minutes. Remove from heat. Stir in dill and lemon juice; season soup with salt.

Nutrition Info

Calories 529, Carbohydrates 34 g, Fat 31 g, Protein 28 g, Saturated Fat 8 g, Sodium 491 mg

Roasted cauliflower, fennel and ginger soup

Point Values: 19

Ingredients

- 1 red onion quartered & 4 garlic cloves
- ½ head large cauliflower (cut into florets) & 2 fennel bulbs chopped and cored
- 500 gms stock of choice & 3 tbs hummus (optional, I had this in the fridge)
- 1 TBS Golden Gut Blend (or use 1 tsp tumeric and pinch cinnamon and black pepper) & 1 tsp sage leaves
- pinch fennel seeds & 2 tbs wheat free tamari
- 2 tbs lemon & 1 knob ginger (peeled)

Instructions

- First Preheat oven to 200 degrees Celsius
- Next On a baking tray place red onion, garlic cloves, cauliflower and the fennel.
- Then Bake for 30-35 minutes until crispy.
- After that Remove from the oven and place in a blender with remaining ingredients.
- In the next step Blend until creamy.
- Pour into heavy bottomed saucepan and place on stovetop.
- Heat through on low to allow flavours to meld.
- Season to taste.
- Let cool slightly and serve warm.
- Finally Decorate with fennel fronds.

Nutrition Info

Calories 378, Carbohydrates 42 g, Fat 45 g, Protein 32 g, Saturated Fat 7 g, Sodium 217 mg

Homemade Vegetarian Chili

Prep/Cook Time: 1 hour, 4 to 6 servings
Point Values: 13

Ingredients

- 2 tablespoons extra-virgin olive oil & 1 medium red onion, chopped
- 1 large red bell pepper, chopped & 2 medium carrots, chopped
- 2 ribs celery, chopped & ½ teaspoon salt, divided
- 4 cloves garlic, pressed or minced & 2 tablespoons chili powder*
- 2 teaspoons ground cumin & 1 ½ teaspoons smoked paprika*
- 1 teaspoon dried oregano & 1 large can (28 ounces) or 2 small cans (15 ounces each) diced tomatoes**, with their juices
- 2 cans (15 ounces each) black beans, rinsed and drained & 1 can (15 ounces) pinto beans, rinsed and drained
- 2 cups vegetable broth or water & 1 bay leaf
- 2 tablespoons chopped fresh cilantro, plus more for garnishing & 1 to 2 teaspoons sherry vinegar or red wine vinegar or lime juice, to taste
- Garnishes: chopped cilantro, sliced avocado, tortilla chips, sour cream or crème fraîche, grated cheddar cheese, etc.

Instructions

- At first In a large Dutch oven or heavy-bottomed pot over medium heat, warm the olive oil until shimmering. Next Add the chopped onion, bell pepper, carrot, celery and ¼ teaspoon of the salt. Then Stir to combine and cook, stirring occasionally, until the vegetables are tender and the onion is translucent, about 7 to 10 minutes.
- In the next stepAdd the garlic, chili powder, cumin, smoked paprika and oregano. Cook until fragrant while stirring constantly, about 1 minute.
- Add the diced tomatoes and their juices, the drained black beans and pinto beans, vegetable broth and bay leaf. Stir to combine and let the mixture come to a simmer. Continue cooking, stirring occasionally and reducing heat as necessary to maintain a gentle simmer, for 30 minutes. Remove the chili from the heat.
- For the best texture and flavor, transfer 1 ½ cups of the chili to a blender, making sure to get some of the liquid portion. Securely fasten the lid and blend until smooth (watch out for hot steam), then pour the blended mixture back into the pot. (Or, you can blend the chili briefly with an immersion blender, or mash the chili with a potato masher until it reaches a thicker, more chili-like consistency.)
- Finally Add the chopped cilantro, stir to blend, and then mix in the vinegar, to taste. Add salt to taste, too — I added ¼ teaspoon more at this point. Divide the mixture into individual bowls and serve with garnishes of your choice. This chili will keep well in the

refrigerator for about 4 days or you can freeze it for longer-term storage

Nutrition Info

Calories 324, Carbohydrates 26 g, Fat 29 g, Protein 33 g

Baked Tilapia Recipe with Pecan Rosemary Topping

Prep/Cook Time: 33 mins, Serves 4
Point Values: 3

Ingredients

- 1/3 cup chopped raw pecans & 1/3 cup whole wheat panko breadcrumbs
- 2 tsp chopped fresh rosemary & 1/2 tsp coconut palm sugar or brown sugar
- 1/8 tsp salt & 1 pinch cayenne pepper
- 1 1/2 tsp olive oil , 1 egg white & 4 (4 oz. each) tilapia fillets

Instructions

- At first Preheat oven to 350 degrees F.
- Next In a small baking dish, stir together pecans, breadcrumbs, rosemary, coconut palm sugar, salt and cayenne pepper. Add the olive oil and toss to coat the pecan mixture.
- Then Bake until the pecan mixture is light golden brown, 7 to 8 minutes.
- After that Increase the heat to 400 degrees F. Coat a large glass baking dish with cooking spray.
- In a shallow dish, whisk the egg white. Working with one tilapia at a time, dip the fish in the egg white and then the pecan mixture, lightly coating each side. Place the fillets in the prepared baking dish.

- Press the remaining pecan mixture into the top of the tilapia fillets.
- Finally Bake until the tilapia is just cooked through, about 10 minutes. Serve.

Nutrition Info

Calories 222.4 cal, Calories from fat 90, Total Fat 10.8g, Saturated Fat 1.4g, Cholesterol 55.0mg, Sodium 153.3mg

Turkey & Quinoa Stuffed Peppers

Prep/Cook Time: 1 hour 20 mins, Servings: 4
Point Values: 6

Ingredients:

- 3 large yellow peppers & 1.25lb extra lean ground turkey
- 1 C diced mushrooms & 1/4 C diced sweet onion
- 1 C chopped fresh spinach & 2 teaspoons minced garlic
- 1 C (1 8oz can) tomato sauce, 1 C chicken broth & 1 C dry quinoa

Instructions:

- At first In a small saucepan, start the quinoa and cook according to package Instructions (usually about 15 minutes).
- Next While the quinoa cooks, saute the vegetables in a pan with a little butter or olive oil.
- Then after about 5 minutes or so, add the ground turkey and garlic to the vegetables. Cook over medium heat. Once the turkey is mostly cooked though, add in the tomato sauce and about half of the chicken broth. Let simmer until the turkey is fully cooked and some of the excess liquid has cooked off.
- After that Preheat the oven to 400.
- In the next step While the turkey mixture simmers, prep your bell peppers. Wash the peppers, cut them in half, and remove the stem & seeds. Spray a 9×13

baking pan with cooking spray and place the cut bell peppers in the pan (open side up).
- Once the quinoa is done cooking, dump it into the pan with the turkey & vegetables. Stir together. Then, stuff each bell pepper with the mixture. Make sure they are nice & full! If you're opting for cheese, then top with just enough cheese to barely cover the mixture (if you put too much on, it will get super messy in the oven!). Pour the rest of the chicken broth into the base of the pan (so around the peppers, not over them).turkey & quinoa stuffed yellow peppers
- Finally Cover with foil and bake at 400 for about 30-35 minutes. Serve warm & eat up!
- They are sooooo good!

Nutrition info

264 Calories, 9g Total Fat, 60mg Cholesterol, 722mg Sodium, 22g Carbohydrates, 5g Fiber, 18g Protein

Italian Stuffed Peppers

Prep/Cook Time: 1 hour 15m, Serving:8
Point Values: 6

Ingredients

- 4 medium to large green or red bell peppers & 1 1/2 pounds lean ground beef
- 1 cup chopped onion & 1 cup cooked rice
- 2 teaspoons McCormick® Perfect Pinch® Italian Seasoning & 1/2 teaspoon McCormick® Garlic Powder
- 1/2 teaspoon salt & 1/4 teaspoon McCormick® Black Pepper, Ground
- 2 cans (15 ounces each) tomato sauce, divided & 1/2 cup shredded mozzarella cheese

Instructions

- First Preheat oven to 400°F. Cut off tops of bell peppers. Next Remove seeds and membranes. Then Rinse bell peppers. If necessary, cut thin slice from bottom of each pepper so they stand upright. Set aside.
- After that Brown ground beef and onion in large skillet on medium-high heat. Drain fat. Add rice, Italian seasoning, garlic powder, salt and pepper; mix until well blended.
- In the next step Pour 1 can of the tomato sauce into bottom of 9-inch square baking dish. Stuff peppers with beef mixture. Place stuffed peppers upright in baking dish. Pour remaining can tomato sauce over stuffed peppers. Cover tightly with foil.
- Finally Bake 35 to 45 minutes or until peppers are tender. Remove foil. Sprinkle stuffed peppers with cheese. Bake 5 minutes longer or until cheese is melted. Cut stuffed peppers in half. Spoon sauce in dish over each half to serve.

Nutrition info

245 Calories, 9g Total Fat, 56mg Cholesterol, 955mg Sodium, 19g Carbohydrates, 4g Fiber, 22g Protein

Mediterranean Tuna-Spinach Salad

Prep/Cook Time: 10 m
Point Values: 5

Ingredients

- 1½ tablespoons tahini & 1½ tablespoons lemon juice
- 1½ tablespoons water & 1 5-ounce can chunk light tuna in water, drained
- 4 Kalamata olives, pitted and chopped & 2 tablespoons feta cheese
- 2 tablespoons parsley , 2 cups baby spinach & 1 medium orange, peeled or sliced

Instructions

- Whisk tahini, lemon juice and water together in a bowl. Add tuna, olives, feta and parsley; stir to combine. Serve the tuna salad over 2 cups spinach, with the orange on the side.

Nutrition Info

Serving size: 1 cup tuna salad, 2 cups spinach & 1 orange
Per serving: 375 calories; 21 g fat(5 g sat); 6 g fiber; 26 g

DESSERTS RECIPES

Frozen Blueberry Bites

Prep/Cook Time: 30 mins, Servings: 4
Point Values: 9

Ingredients

- 8 ounces vanilla yogurt
- 2 teaspoons lemon juice
- 1 pint blueberries

Instructions

- First In a large bowl, carefully mix the blueberries, lemon juice and yogurt together. (Be gentle; you don't want any berries to get squished.)
- Next Scoop out the yogurt-coated blueberries one by one and place them on a baking sheet lined with parchment paper.
- Finally Freeze for two hours before serving.

Nutrition Info

Calories: 204kcal, Carbohydrates: 33g, Protein: 30g, Fat: 12g, Saturated Fat: 11g, Cholesterol: 123mg

One-Ingredient Watermelon Sorbet

Prep/Cook Time: 4 hr
Point Values: 10

Ingredient

- 1 seedless watermelon, peeled and cubed

Instructions

o At first Arrange the watermelon cubes in an even layer on a baking sheet. Next Transfer the baking sheet to thefreezer and freeze until the watermelon is solid, about 2 hours.
o Next Working in batches, transfer the watermelon cubes to a blender or food processor and puree until smooth.
o Then Divide the puree among two loaf pans (or put it all in one deep baking dish), packing it down as you add more on top.
o In the next step Transfer the pans to the freezer. Freeze until the sorbet is scoopable, 1 to 2 hours more.
o Finally To serve, scoop the sorbet into dishes and eat immediately.

Nutrition Info

339 calories, 2g fat, 86g carbs, 7g protein, 70g sugars

Apple Chips

Prep/Cook Time: 4 hrs, Servings: 3 cups
Point Values: 2

Ingredients

- 3 large sweet — crisp apples, such as Honeycrisp, Fuji, Jazz, or Pink Lady
- 3/4 teaspoon ground cinnamon

Instructions

o At first Place racks in the upper and lower thirds of your oven and preheat your oven to 200 degrees F. Next Line two baking sheets with parchment paper or a silpat mat.

o Then Wash the apples. With an apple corer, very small cookie cutter, or the round side of a metal piping tip, core the apples (you can also skip this step if you don't mind a few seeds in the chips). With a mandolin (recommended) or a very sharp knife, slice the apples horizontally into 1/8 inch-thick rounds.

o Arrange the apples in a single layer on the prepared baking sheets. Sprinkle with cinnamon. Bake for 1 hour in the upper and lower thirds of the oven. Remove the baking sheets and switch the pans' position on the upper and lower racks. Continue baking for 1 to 1 1/2 additional hours, until a single apple chip removed from the oven is crisp when set out at room temperature for 2 to 3 minutes (to test the apple chips, remove a single apple slice but let the others continue baking).Finally Once you are happy with the crispness (the Prep/Cook Time will vary based on the thickness of your slice and the type of apple), turn off the oven and let the apples sit in the oven for 1 hour as it cools down to crisp further (unless you fear you overcooked them, in which case remove the pan immediately and let it sit at room temperature).

Nutrition Info

Calories: 65, Sodium: 2mg, Carbohydrates: 18g, Fiber: 5g, Sugar: 11g

Strawberry-Orange Sorbet

Prep/Cook Time: 5 mins, Serves: 3 cups
Point Values:

Ingredients
- 1 pound frozen strawberries
- 1 cup orange juice (or 1 cup of coconut water)

Instructions
- At first Add strawberries to a food processor and mix until the fruit is reduced to flakes, about 1 to 2 minutes.
- Next Add orange juice (or coconut water) and continue to mix until you obtain a smooth frozen puree. You might have to push the mixture down the sides of the food processor a few times.
- Finally Serve immediately as a soft serve, freeze for about 45 minutes to 1 hour for a sorbet consistency, or pour into popsicle molds and freeze overnight.

Nutrition Info : Calories: 222kcal, Carbohydrates: 8g, Protein: 34g, Fat: 8g, Saturated Fat: 4.5g, Cholesterol: 30mg

Paleo Pineapple Upside Down Cake

Prep/Cook Time: 30 mins, Serving: 1

Point Values: 6

Ingredients

- 1 cup almond flour & 2 eggs
- ½ tsp baking powder & 5 tbsp raw honey
- 3 tbsp liquid coconut oil & 1 tsp pure vanilla extract
- 2 slices of fresh pineapple, each ½ inch thick & 15 fresh or frozen sweet cherries

Instructions

- At first Preheat oven to 350 F. Next Peel and core the pineapple slices. Then Place 1 ½ tbsp of raw honey in an 8" cast iron skillet or round cake tin. Arrange the pineapple rings and sweet cherries on the honey in a decorative pattern. Place the skillet in the oven and cook for 15 minutes.
- In the next step Mix almond flour with baking powder. In a medium bowl cream the eggs with remaining honey. Add the coconut oil and mix to combine. Add the almond mixture and mix well to combine. Remove the skillet from the oven and pour batter over the top of the pineapple rings and smooth it out. Return in the oven and bake for 35 minutes.
- Finally Remove from the oven and leave to stand for 10 minutes, then turn out onto a plate. Serve with more fresh sweet cherries.

Nutrition Info : Calories 213, Carbohydrates 21.6 g, Fat 13.2 g, Sugar 17.4 g, Protein 4.9 g, Fiber 2.4 g

Chocolate Cherry Chia Pudding

Prep/Cook Time: 4 hours 10 mins, Servings: 4
Point Values: 5

Ingredients

- 1 1/2 cup non-dairy milk (almond/ coconut/ hemp are my favourites) & 1/4 cup chia seeds (look for powdered chia seeds if you want a smooth texture)
- 3 tablespoons raw cacao powder & 2-3 tablespoons pure maple syrup or honey
- 1/2 cup cherries, pitted and sliced + extra for plating & Additional toppings : extra cherries, raw cacao nibs, dark chocolate shavings (use 70% dark chocolate or higher)

Instructions

- At first In a bowl or mason jar, stir together the first 4 ingredients: milk, chia seeds, raw cacao and maple syrup and refrigerate for at least 4 hours or overnight. (If using a Mason Jar, simply close the lid and shake!)
- Finally Just before serving, separate into 4 serving dishes, top with sliced cherries and garnish with raw cacao chips, dark chocolate shavings and extra whole cherries and enjoy!

Nutrition Info : Calories: 170kcal, Carbohydrates: 19g, Protein: 12g, Fat: 7g, Saturated Fat: 7g, Cholesterol: 40mg

SMOOTHIES AND DRINKS

Anti-Inflammatory Pumpkin Smoothie

Prep/Cook Time: 30 mins, Servings: 2
Point Values: 4

Ingredients

- 2 cups pumpkin & 1 banana
- 1/2 cup plain yogurt & 1 1/2 tbsp. agave syrup

Instructions

- First Peel the pumpkin, cut in quarters and remove seeds. Next Cut de-seeded pumpkin into smaller pieces and press.
- Then Peel and cut banana, mix with yogurt and press.
- Finally Add agave syrup, mix well and serve.

Nutrition Info

Calories 138 Calories from Fat 18, Total Fat 2g, Saturated Fat 1g, Trans Fat 0g, Cholesterol 8mg, Sodium 30mg, Total Carbohydrate 29g, Dietary Fiber 2g, Sugars 16g, Protein 4g

Anti-Inflammatory Turmeric Ginger Green Smoothie for Weight Loss

Prep/Cook Time: 5 minutes, Servings: 1
Point Values: 4

Ingredients

- 1 cup light coconut milk or unsweetened almond milk & 1 cup chopped fresh kale
- 1 cup chopped fresh pineapple, frozen & ½ cup chopped mango, frozen
- 1 tbsp lemon juice & ½ tbsp fresh ginger, grated
- ¼ to ½ tsp ground turmeric (to taste), pinch of ground black pepper & ½ to 1 cup ice

Instructions

- Place all the ingredients in a blender and blend until smooth.
- Serve immediately.

Nutrition Info

Calories: 181, Carbohydrates: 21.1 g, Fat: 3.7 g, Sugar: 18.3 g, Protein: 4.1 g

Anti-Inflammatory Blueberry Smoothie

Prep/Cook Time: 5 mins, Servings: 1
Point Values: 9

Ingredients

- 1 cup almond milk
- 1 frozen banana
- 2/3 - 1 cup frozen blueberries
- 2 handfuls spinach or leafy greens
- 1 T almond butter
- 1/4 tsp cinnamon
- 1/8 - 1/4 tsp cayenne start light and add as desired
- 1 tsp maca powder optional

Instructions

o Combine all ingredients in a high powered blender and blend until smooth. Serve immediately.

Nutrition Info

Calories: 340kcal, Carbohydrates: 55g, Protein: 9g, Fat: 13g, Saturated Fat: 1g, Sodium: 376mg, Potassium: 991mg, Fiber: 11g, Sugar: 30g

Food Babe's Ginger Berry Anti-Inflammatory Smoothie

Prep/Cook Time: 5 mins, Servings: 1
Point Values: 2

Ingredients

- 3 tablespoons hemp protein powder & 2 inch piece of ginger (peeled if not organic)
- 2 cups of leafy greens (kale, collards, romaine, spinach, chard, etc.) & 1 cup of celery
- 1 cup of mixed frozen berries of your choice (strawberries, blueberries, cranberries, etc) & ½ cup filtered water

Instructions

- At first Place all ingredients in a blender and blend for 1 min or until smooth
- Finally Serve immediately or store in airtight container for up to 1 day

Nutrition Info

Calories 172, Calories from Fat 44, Total Fat 2g, Saturated Fat 12g, Trans Fat 0g, Cholesterol 40mg, Protein 21g

Anti-Inflammatory Smoothie

Prep/Cook Time: 10 minutes, Servings: 2
Point Values: 7

Ingredients

- 2 cups baby kale & 1 small beet (peeled and chopped)
- 1 cup water & 1 orange (peeled)
- 2 cups mixed berries (frozen) & 1 cup pineapple (frozen)
- 1 tablespoon fresh ginger (grated or chopped) & 1 tablespoon coconut oil

Instructions

- First Place baby kale, beet, water, and orange into a blender.
- Next Puree until smooth.
- Then Add remaining ingredients.
- Finally Blend again until smooth.

Notes : Carrots can be substituted for the beets, Mango can be substituted for the pineapple.

Nutrition Info : Calories: 264, Sugar: 30g, Sodium: 66g, Fat: 8g, Saturated Fat: 6g, Carbohydrates: 47g, Fiber: 8g, Protein: 5g, Cholesterol: 0g

Golden Milk Protein Smoothie

Prep/Cook Time: 5 minutes, Servings: 1
Point Values: 6

Ingredients

- 1 cup frozen mango chunks & ½ frozen banana
- 1/2 cup plain Greek yogurt (use a dairy-free substitute if needed) & 1/2 teaspoon ground cinnamon
- 1/2 teaspoon ground turmeric or 1 Tablespoon peeled and grated fresh turmeric & 1/4 teaspoon ground ginger or 1/2 Tablespoons peeled and grated fresh ginger
- 1 cup unsweetened vanilla almond milk (or your favorite milk) & pinch of black pepper

Instructions

o Blend everything together in a high powered blender until smooth. Pour into a cup and enjoy.

Notes : Feel free to swap the frozen mango for frozen pineapple or do a mixture of both!

Nutrition Info :
Calories: 234, Sugar: 31g, Sodium: 231mg, Fat: 3g, Carbohydrates: 42g, Fiber: 6g, Protein: 12g

SNACKS RECIPES

Ginger Fried Cabbage and Carrots

Prep/Cook Time: 13 mins, Serves: 4
Point Values: 9

Ingredients

- 2 tbsp. oil & 1 tbsp. ginger, minced
- 2 garlic cloves, crushed
- 4 c green cabbage, shredded
- 2 carrots, julienned or grated (about 1.5-2 c) & 1 tbsp. apple cider vinegar
- 1 tbsp. coconut aminos & ¼ c green onion, chopped

Instructions

- At first In a large skillet, heat oil on medium high. Next Add garlic and ginger. Then Cook until fragrant, about one minute.
- After that Add cabbage and carrot. Cook until soft, about 6-8 minutes.
- Finally Remove the cabbage and carrot mix from the heat. Stir in coconut aminos, vinegar, and green onion. Serve.

Nutrition Info

Calories 342, Total Fat 24g, Saturated Fat 6g, Trans Fat 8g, Cholesterol 0mg, Protein 33g

Turmeric Coconut Flour Muffins Recipe

Prep/Cook Time: 30 mins, Serves:8 muffins
Point Values: 2

Ingredients
- 6 large eggs & ½ cup unsweetened coconut milk
- 1/4 cup maple syrup & 1 t vanilla extract
- ¾ cup + 2 T coconut flour & ½ t baking soda
- 2 t turmeric, ½ t ginger powder & Pinch of salt and pepper

Instructions

- At first Preheat oven to 350°F. Next Prepare a muffin tin with 8 muffin liners.
- Then In a large mixing bowl, add eggs, milk, maple syrup, and vanilla extract. Mix until it's well-combined and the eggs begin to bubble.
- After that In a small bowl, sift together coconut flour, baking soda, turmeric, ginger powder, pepper, and salt.
- Slowly stir the dry ingredients into the wet ones, until the batter is smooth and thick.
- Transfer the batter to a prepared muffin tin, dividing the batter evenly.
- Bake for 25 minutes, until slightly browned around the edges.
- Finally Remove muffins from the oven, and transfer to a wire rack to cool.

Nutrition Info : Calories 160, Calories from Fat 22, Total Fat 4g, Saturated Fat 4g, Trans Fat 8g, Protein 9g

Baked Veggie Turmeric Nuggets (Freeze-Friendly)

Prep/Cook Time: 35 mins, Serves: 24 nuggets

Point Values: 5

Ingredients
- 2 cups cauliflower florets & 2 cups broccoli florets
- 1 cup carrots, coarsely chopped & 1 t garlic, minced
- 1/2 t ground turmeric & 1/4 t sea salt
- 1/4 t black pepper, 1/2 cup almond meal & 1 large pasture-raised egg

Instructions
- At first Preheat the oven to 400°F and line the baking sheet with parchment paper.
- Next Combine the broccoli, cauliflower, carrots, garlic, turmeric, sea salt and black pepper in a food processor. Pulse until fine.
- Then Add the almond meal and egg, and pulse until just mixed in.
- After that Transfer to a mixing bowl. Scoop out the mixture by the tablespoon and use your hands to form into circular discs. Place onto the lined baking sheet.
- Finally Bake for 25 minutes, flipping after 15 minutes. Serve with Paleo ranch sauce for dipping.

Nutrition Info : Calories 190, Calories from Fat 10, Total Fat 12g, Protein 16g

AIP / Paleo Sweet n' Sour Hibiscus Ginger Gelatin Gummies

Prep/Cook Time: 12 mins, Serves: 28 gummies

Point Values: 1

Ingredients

- 1 cup water, 3 TBSP hibiscus flowers cut & 1½ TBSP honey
- 1 TSP ginger juice & 2 TBSP gelatin powder (Great Lakes - red can)

Instructions

- First Bring water to a boil in a small pot.
- Next Remove from the heat and add hibiscus flowers.
- Then Cover and infuse for 5 minutes.
- After that Drain the flowers with a small strainer.
- In the next step Return the liquid to the pot, add honey, ginger, and mix well with a whisk.
- Sprinkle the gelatin over the liquid's surface and wait for the gelatin to soften and dissolve. After a few minutes, mix with the whisk to make sure that the gelatin is well dissolved without any clumps.
- Pour immediately in the silicon mold (or a rectangular baking dish lined with parchment paper).
- Let cool down and place in the fridge for at least 2 hours.
- Finally To unmold your gummies, simply push on the underside of the mold with your fingers and the gummies will pop out.
- Bon appétit!

Nutrition Info : Calories 222, Calories from Fat 20, Total Fat 2g, Saturated Fat 0g, Trans Fat 0g, Cholesterol 0mg, Protein 6g

Vanilla Turmeric Orange Juice

Prep/Cook Time: 5 mins, Serves:2

Point Values: 10

Ingredients

- 3 oranges, peeled + quartered & 1 cup unsweetened almond milk
- 1 t vanilla extract & ½ t cinnamon
- ¼ t turmeric & Pinch of pepper

Instructions

- Place all the ingredients in a blender.
- Blend until smooth, then pour into a glass and serve.

Nutrition Info

Calories 150, Calories from Fat 30, Protein 22g

Spicy Tuna Rolls

Prep/Cook Time: 10 minutes, Servings: 6
Point Values: 3

Ingredients

- 1 medium cucumber & 1 pouch StarKist Selects E.V.O.O. Wild-Caught Yellowfin Tuna
- 1 tsp hot sauce & 1/8 tsp salt
- 1/8 tsp pepper, 1/16 tsp ground cayenne & 2 slices avocado, diced

Materials

12 toothpicks

Instructions

- First Using a mandolin, thinly slice the cucumber lengthwise. Next Once cucumber has been sliced down to where seeds appear, flip cucumber over and thinly slice the opposite side. Discard outermost slices of cucumber and any slices where seeds are present. Pat dry the remaining slices (6 total are needed) with a paper towel. Set aside.
- Then To a small mixing bowl, add tuna, hot sauce, salt, pepper, and cayenne. Mix until ingredients are thoroughly incorporated.
- Finally One slice at a time, spoon tuna mixture across cucumber slices, leaving one inch on each side. Place one piece of avocado on top of tuna and carefully roll cucumber up, securing the end with 2 toothpicks.

Nutrition Info

Calories Per Serving: 122, Total Fat 8.8g, Total Carbohydrate 2g, Dietary Fiber 1.4g, Protein 9.5g

VEGETARIAN RECIPES

Thai Coconut Soup with Bok Choy & Mushrooms

Prep/Cook Time: 15 mins, Servings: 3-4
Point Values: 8

Ingredients:

- 1 tbsp coconut oil (or your choice of oil) & 1 tbsp freshly minced ginger
- 10 oz cremimi mushrooms - thinly sliced & 1 tbsp Season with Spice's Thai BBQ Seasoning
- 1/2 tsp Season with Spice's Turmeric Powder, or more to taste & 2 1/2 cups vegetable broth, or water
- 12 oz package of firm silken tofu - cut into small cubes & 1/3 cup to 1/2 cup coconut milk
- Sea salt to season (I used our Sweet Ginger Sea Salt) & 4-5 bunches of baby bok choy - thinly sliced

Instructions

o First Heat coconut oil in a pot or large skillet, over medium fire. Next Add half of the minced ginger and cook until aromatic, about 30 seconds. Then Add in sliced mushrooms and cook for about 4 minutes. When the liquid begin to evaporate, add in our Thai BBQ Seasoning and turmeric powder. Stir to mix in.

o Add in broth/water and tofu cubes, and bring it to a boil. Add in the remaining minced ginger. Lower heat to medium, and add in coconut milk. Stir gently to combine. Let cook for another minute. Season with our

Sweet Ginger Sea Salt. Taste, and adjust any seasonings to your taste. If you like the soup to be a richer consistency, just add in a bit more of the coconut milk.
o Remove from heat. Finally Stir in the bok choy to lightly wilt. Serve hot or warm.

Notes:

- The soup keeps well for 2-3 days in the refrigerator. When reheating, feel free to add in more liquid or coconut milk if the soup gets too thick.
- For an even fresher tasting bok choy in the soup, add them in right at the table before you dig in.

Nutrition Info

Calories Per Serving: 222, Total Fat 14g, Total Carbohydrate 23g, Dietary Fiber 6g, Protein 26g

Anti-Inflammatory Soup (GF/DF)

Prep/Cook Time: 30 mins, Servings: 3
Point Values: 3

Ingredients

- 5 carrots & 1 raw beetroot (not the cooked kind if you can help it)
- 2 sticks of celery & 1 sweet potato
- 1 tbsp. of turmeric & 1 thumb sized piece of ginger, grated or chopped finely.
- 1 garlic clove chopped. & 1 tablespoon of vegan bouillon powder (or a powdered stock cube that has no MSG, Gluten or dairy)
- 1 tablespoon & 1 tablespoon of coconut cream or a dairy-free alternative (use fat free dairy free yoghurt for syn free)

Instructions

- At first Wash and chop all the vegetables and place in boiling water. Then add the ginger, garlic, turmeric and bouillon powder.
- Next Once boiled, cover and simmer on a low heat and cook for 25 minutes.
- Once vegetables are soft, allow to cool for ten minutes.
- Add ingredients to your blender (I used my trusty nutribullet), alongside coconut cream/dairy free milk alternative to add creaminess (note coconut cream will

make it extra creamy, milk alternatives will make it slightly thinner) and blend for 30 seconds.
- o For an extra health kick sprinkle with protein Powder
- o Finally Serve with seed crackers or a hearty dose of gluten free bread!

Nutrition Info

Calories: 327, Total Fat 8g, Total Carbohydrate 4g, Dietary Fiber 8g, Protein 11g

Turmeric Latte

Prep/Cook Time: 5 mins, Servings: 1
Point Values: 7

Ingredients

- 250 mls / 1 cup homemade or unsweetened almond milk & 1-2 tsp coconut sugar / honey / other sweetener
- 1/2 tsp turmeric & 1/2 tsp cinnamon
- 1/4 tsp ground ginger / small piece of fresh ginger grated & Pinch of black pepper (to support absorbtion of the curcumin)
- Optional but recommended if using shop bought almond milk: 1/2 tbsp coconut oil

Instructions

- First Warm the almond milk in a pan on the stove or in the microwave on high for 2 minutes.
- Finally Add the remaining ingredients and whisk or blend until frothy &Enjoy!

Nutrition Info : Calories: 444, Fat: 8g, Sodium: 135mg, Carbohydrates: 30g, Fiber: 3.3g, Sugar: 1.2g, Protein: 22g

Turmeric Roasted Cauliflower

Prep/Cook Time: 30 minutes, Servings: 6
Point Values: 9

Ingredients
- 1 large head cauliflower, cut into 1 inch florets {about 1 1/2 to 2 pounds} & 3 garlic cloves, minced
- 3 Tablespoons olive oil & 1 teaspoon turmeric
- 1/2 teaspoon cumin & 1/2 teaspoon paprika
- 1/4 teaspoon coriander & 1/4 teaspoon red pepper flakes
- 1 teaspoon kosher salt & 1/2 teaspoon ground black pepper

Garnish : Cilantro

Instructions
- At first Preheat the oven to 450 degrees F.
- Next Cut the cauliflower into 1-inch florets and place them in a large mixing bowl with the minced garlic.
- Then In a small mixing bowl combine the olive oil, turmeric, cumin, paprika, coriander, crushed red pepper, salt and pepper and stir. Drizzle the olive oil mixture over the cauliflower and toss to coat.
- On a large baking sheet evenly spread the cauliflower.
- Roast in the oven for 25-30 minutes or until the cauliflower is tender and starting to brown on the ends.
- Finally Serve warm with cilantro.

Nutrition Info : Calories: 154, Fat: 20g, Sodium: 148mg, Carbohydrates: 22g, Fiber: 33g, Sugar: 12g, Protein: 47g

Pesto Broccoli Sweet Potato Rice Casserole

Prep/Cook Time: 55 mins, Servings: 1
Point Values: 8

Ingredients
For the pesto:
- 2.5 cups basil leaves, packed & 3 tbsp of pine nuts
- 1/4 cup of olive oil (if you like it thicker, less olive oil) & 5 cranks of the sea salt grinder
- 5 cranks of the peppercorn grinder & 1 large clove of garlic minced
- For the rest: & 2 cups small broccoli florets
- 1 large sweet potato (350g), peeled, Blade C & pepper, to taste
- 1/3 cup low-sodium vegetable broth & 1.5 cups shredded mozzarella (optional)

Instructions
- First Preheat the oven to 400 degrees.
- Next Place all of the ingredients for the pesto into a food processor and pulse until smooth. Taste and just, if necessary. Pour half of the pesto out into a bowl and add in the broccoli. Toss until broccoli is coated with the pesto. Set the broccoli and remaining pesto aside.
- Then In the bottom of the casserole, spread out a thin layer of pesto. Then, spread out a layer of the sweet potato rice. Then, add the broccoli. Then, add the rest of the rice to cover the broccoli. Drizzle the remaining pesto over the rice. Then, pour over the vegetable broth. Season with pepper. If using mozzarella, spread over in an even layer over the rice to cover.
- Finally Cover the casserole with tinfoil and bake for 40 minutes.

Nutrition Info
Calories: 262, Fat: 3g, Sodium: 230mg, Carbohydrates: 43g, Fiber: 3g, Sugar: 1.2g, Protein: 27g